Talitha Koum

Girl Get UP!

By: Tammira Sheriece Sanders

Dedication

I would like to dedicate this book to the six-year-old me. The enemy tried to bury you, but he didn't know you were a seed! To my answered prayer, my husband Joshua, thank you so much for coming alongside me and pushing me. You have helped me birth this book in more ways than one and I truly bless God for your life. To the girls Addison, Aaurlow, Marcella and Jael always remember that you are fearfully and wonderfully made and that there are souls attached to your voice. And whenever the enemy tries to attack you in any way, hear that still small voice say Talitha Koum "Little Girl Arise".

Table of Contents

1. Her Innocence Stolen — 1
2. Broken Home / Faulty Foundations — 7
3. Get In Where You Fit In — 11
4. Rebellion as the Sin of Witchcraft — 15
5. Busting It (Hell) Wide Open — 19
6. "Love" Is Blind — 23
7. Unveiled — 47
8. Promise Fulfilled — 67

Chapter 1
Her Innocence Stolen

I grew up in a two-parent home. My mom and my dad were in the home with me as I grew up. This did not exempt me from the trials and tribulations that came along in this life. Don't believe me? Come on this journey with me as I share with you, my story.

I grew up going over to my grandmother's house often. I'm the youngest of three children and my mother and father always worked. Therefore, from a very young age of 3 years old I started to go over to my grandmother's house for school. My grandmother was a teacher assistant in an elementary school. So, I spent Monday through Friday over there. These early years of my life were building a foundation that I would one day later in life have to stand on.

If the foundations be destroyed, what can the righteous do?

Psalm 11:3 (KJV)

So, let's fast forward to 1993 – 1994, I'm between the ages of five and six. I was always a happy and loving child. I still am that way till this day. Anyway, as I previously stated, I was at my grandparents often and my great grandmother also lived there. I would get dropped off there from the school bus during the weekdays. I'd always go in and watch TV or read a book. I loved reading back then. My brother's friends often came over there from the neighborhood. I mean my grandparents' place was like a family house so to say. The kids around the way knew they could get food and love whenever they came by. Well, my brother had this one friend named Shawn that would hang around with him. I had seen him around many times with my brother over my grandparents' house. I'm about six years old so I'm playing as usual and I'm sure just wanting to be around my brother. He's eight years older than I am, so I was just being a little sister. Well, nobody knew it at the time but I guess this kid Shawn had started to look at me inappropriately. One day Shawn caught me in a room by myself over my grandparents' house and told me to come straight home from school and meet him in this same room. He said not to tell anyone, so I didn't. I remember coming home from school to my grandparents and doing just as he said. I went to that room and waited for him as he asked me to. Y'all to this day I do not know how it got to this point. He had to have groomed me in some way shape or form. But I remember him coming there and I believe I am the one who answered the door for him. He got there and told me to go to the bathroom and then come back to the room. When I got back to the room, he proceeded to coerce me into molesting me. I was six years old, a baby. I didn't know any better. I remember it being extremely painful. Then He did it again and again. I can't recall how long it took place, but I do remember one day going to the emergency room. After that it is truly a blur. That was it, my innocence stolen. The molestation led me down a path of promiscuity and sexual perversion but God. Keep reading to see the redemptive power of God.

Chapter 2
Broken Home / Faulty Foundations

Growing up I had both parents in my house. My mom and dad were married around the time my older brother was the age of two. I also have an older sister and then yes, I am the baby. I was a normal little girl up until my innocence was stolen. I loved dolls and babies, you know the normal things that little girls my age liked. At the same time though because of the molestation that happened a year or so prior to now, I had developed an addiction to masturbation. I couldn't have been no older than 6 or 7 years old. I would do it all the time unbeknownst to my mom and dad. If and whenever I had the opportunity, I would touch myself inappropriately. I would watch sex scenes of certain movies repeatedly to arouse myself. This is why it's so important to monitor what your children watch. So sadly, I did this all in secret and didn't know how to stop. I did know that it was wrong, but I didn't know what to do about it. I couldn't ask my mom about it cause boy would I have really been in trouble. I was addicted and had a spirit of perversion and lust on me at the tender age of 7 years. All the while dealing with masturbation a year or so passes and then my home is just utterly broken. My mom finds out about some infidelity with my dad. They are now arguing almost every day. My dad would raise his voice at my mom, and it would scare the beejeebies out of me. I believe this might be when the spirit of fear truly gripped me. I would be so afraid at bedtime when my dad hadn't come home yet because I knew that they were going to argue. And most times they did. I wouldn't be able to really get rest some nights because I was just so afraid someone would get hurt. Then I would go to school and end up in the nurse's office because I would get a pain in my ankle that wouldn't go away with medicine. I know now that was because it was spiritual and you can't medicate demons, Amen. You gotta cast them out!! Anyway, I would be in the office, and they would ask "what's wrong" and I wouldn't say because you know that saying, "what goes on at this house, stays in this house." May I insert this advice to my African American family and anyone else who holds fast to this trauma filled, generational curse response, that it is retired, and it ends with me and my generation. That saying is demonic and a form of control and manipulation, which is witchcraft. Time passed and the masturbation continued throughout elementary school and so did the arguing and infidelity in my parent's marriage. The devil was trying to have his way but God.

Chapter 3
Get In Where You Fit In

It's the first day of middle school and I sit in the front of the bus by the window. Then this girl gets on the bus after a few stops and sits right next to me. We immediately became best friends. We sat together all the time on the bus and at lunch in school. There was always a bit of contention between us though, because one we were little girls and two, I was finding myself. Or at least I thought I was. During this time in middle school, I struggled to find my identity and where I fit in. I wasn't sure if I fit in with the "in crowd" or the not so in crowd. I was what you would call back then a "friendly Bob".[LOL] Anyways, I owned it though because I was kind of a social butterfly but at the same time very observant of people. So, I would hang out with both crowds. Sadly, each of them would gossip about the other and to fit in so would I sometime. My best friend at the time that I previously mentioned was in the "in crowd". She was a beautiful girl and still is very beautiful to this day. I say she was in the "in crowd" and not we were in the in crowd because this friendship brought on a lot of stress and drama at times. The other girls in the "in crowd" would make fun of me and talk really badly about me. I used to bite my fingernails badly. It was something that had developed, I now know due to the molestation and domestic things going on at home. Nevertheless, these girls and boys a lot of times used that as a point of reference. They would call me nubs and also ugly duckling and compare me to my best friend all of the time. They would always find a way to say that I was following her. This is when I believe that spirit of rejection and spirit of comparison came in. These things also made me question if I was beautiful and good enough. Let's not even talk about boys. All of the boys liked her, and I was okay with that although at times it made me feel rejected. You see there were small seeds that the enemy was planting to try to steal, kill and destroy my identity. We know now though that our identities are in Christ Jesus and not vanity. There is no need to try to fit in when you were destined to be set apart bro or sis. You are his beloved. Amen

Chapter 4
Rebellion as the Sin of Witchcraft

As the years went by and I went on to high school the need to fit in only grew stronger. By this time now though I had grown into my features, so to say. Therefore, the boys in school started to notice me but it wasn't the attention I thought I wanted. I'm well-endowed in the backside area so they were drawn to that. Simply put, it was a spirit of lust and perversion, but I digress. Any attention was good attention though for me because I was struggling with my identity and self-worth. So, I started to date a guy named 'T' my sophomore year of high school. He went to a different school than I did and we had met through my best friend at the time. I had by God's grace "clanked clanked" up until this point of my teenage years. Then I met him, and my mindset went from I'm waiting until I'm married to as long as I'm for sure that I love him, and he loves me. Whew Lord! So, because of peer pressure and honestly manipulation I lost my virginity at the age of 16 going on 17 years old. Oh, how I pray that my life will be a testament to young girls everywhere. It wasn't worth it.

    Now I'm in full-on rebellion. I'm lying to my mom about where I'll be and so on and so forth. Now a year or so has passed and I'm a senior in high school. I had finally made it to what I thought was the "in crowd". I'm smoking weed and having sex with my new boyfriend. I thought I was cool as a fan! All the while the enemy was luring me further and further away from God. I graduated in May 2006 with the thought of going off to college. I was too boy focused though. I have always been someone that loves hard and back then was no different. So, I stayed in my hometown St. Louis, MO and worked some fast-food jobs.

Then in May of 2007 my older cousin Adrienne was getting baptized and invited me to come and be a witness. I was really close to her younger sister Drina, so I went. It was something about this day. I have always loved God up until this point but was young and didn't really make the decision on my own before that day in May. Nevertheless, I'm sitting in Central Baptist Church of off T. E. Huntley and the Lord spoke through the Pastor and it pricked my heart. I re-dedicated my life to Jesus Christ that day. My cousin Drina and I both did, and we got baptized that upcoming Sunday.

So now I started living a life holy, pleasing and acceptable in the sight of God? Well not exactly! I actually continued down the same path for lack of discipleship and the spirit of religion. Let me insert right here that it gets worse before it gets better. But God!

Chapter 5
Busting It (Hell) Wide Open

It's the summer of 2008 and yes, I gave my life to Christ but again I was living in religion and not relationship with Christ Jesus. I was still living a life of fornication and going out drinking and smoking weed. I didn't have a boyfriend at the time, but I did have two guys that I talked to. I want to insert that this was not like me to date and or talk to more than one person at a time, but I was hurt. I had been cheated on by every boyfriend I had up until this point and had decided that no one else was going to get that close to me again. I wasn't going to care enough to get hurt and I was going to love them and leave them. So, I was talking to both of the guys and using them to fulfill the lust of the flesh and the lust of the eye. I was left empty and lonely every time. Most of the time I was drunk when I had these encounters with them after a night out partying/clubbing and then waking up still with the same emotions and reality. Yet, not realizing that every time I laid with them, I was leaving fragments of my soul and taking a piece of them with me

Now some years have went by and it's 2013/2014 and I'm on the East Coast. It was Philly to be exact. I would like to say that the shift in location also completely shifted my mindset to the mind of Christ but no I was still in rebellion. All the while I was praying every night for peace in my heart and also that the Lord would give me a Man of God! Whew I'm so glad that He didn't answer that prayer at the time! As I continued down the path of destruction, fornication, drunkenness and promiscuity I met a guy who I saw potential in to be the man that I thought I wanted. Unfortunately, we were both broken and lost. This relationship would be a turning point in my life. Whether good or bad, keep reading to find out. I also want to make mention that throughout this season of life I was looking for people to fill a void that only Jesus could fill.

Chapter 6
"Love" Is Blind

It's September of 2014 and I got invited to a birthday party by some friends. We all went out to the birthday party, and I love to dance so I found myself on the dance floor dancing to some Dance Hall music (Jamaican music). Y'all I was tearing the dance floor up[lol]. Then that's when I met Dre. We danced for a little and then he asked me where I was from because he thought I was African. He let me know he was Jamaican and then we exchanged numbers as I left the birthday party with my friends. I believe he called me like a day or so afterwards. We had great conversation in the beginning (I met his representative) [lol] no but for real I did. So, we talked and then decided to go out on a few dates. At that time that was a breath of fresh air because most guys had only wanted to smash (yep, I said it). Smash is a colloquialism that was used in the African American culture back then. It meant having sex. Nevertheless, we dated, and I thought I was really doing something by waiting until after about date 5 or so to have sex with him. Also, I had already fallen in love with him by then. The red flags were there though y'all. The first red flag that I had noticed was he didn't tell me right away that he had a child. I found out about it in an unexpected way. I was at his house and I'm not sure exactly what happened but I saw a barrette on the bed. So, I immediately asked him about it and then he was like yea I have a daughter. I wasn't necessarily upset, just caught off guard y'all. I really love kids. Therefore, the child was not a problem. I just didn't know why he hadn't told me upfront. I told him that I felt like he had almost deceived me because what if him having a child was a deal breaker. It would have been hard for me to stop talking to him because I had already grown attached. This is not even taking into account that we'd already had sex with one another, (Soul Tie).

So, we got past that little hiccup or what have you. Then we would have decent conversation and enjoy one another's company but no commitment. There had also been instances where we would be spending time together and I would see the letter V pop up on the call log from his phone on the TV. I asked one time before who that was and why they were calling so late and back-to-back at that. He said she was like a little sister to him. I didn't believe him yet continued our situation-ship. I believe about a year had almost passed by and I'd already had conversations with him about where the situation-ship was going. The conversations never really went anywhere. He would say "I have good intentions for you T". We had plans on going to Florida around September 2015 and we had also signed up to work out at I Love Kickboxing on South Street in Philly.

So it was one evening when we had a class and we were walking up South Street heading to the gym and I saw a white car out of the corner of my eye. Then Dre looks over to me and says something is about to happen, don't freak out. All of sudden we took a few more steps and I see that same white car pull over to the sidewalk. A girl hops out of the car and starts snapping on him. I'm standing off to the side looking at the nonsense take place. I mean y'all she was livid. Then she looked at me and asked me my name. I'm like my name is Tammira. Oh, I forgot to mention this is V that was blowing his phone up all the time. His sister[lol]?!

Well V began to get upset with me and actually wanted to fight me. So, what did I do? I walked clean away from them as he held her foolish behind back from running after me. I walked slowly too y'all. I was like I'm going to let these fools argue because I was practicing as a nurse and was like I have too much to lose. I also thought she was behaving so foolishly because she wanted to fight me. In reality, back then I was like we should be jumping him. Don't judge me y'all, I was not yet walking hand in hand with God.

Anyways I made it to the vehicle, and he came shortly after me. By the time he made it to the car I was absolutely livid. He had the nerve to have a smirk on his face and for some odd reason thought it was ok to try to touch me. It was a bad idea because I was ready to lay hands on him and not the Holy ones[lol]. He went on to say that it's just something that him and his friends do. It was some crazy made up lie y'all[lol]. I can laugh about it now but back then I was not walking with Jesus and wanted to take his head off. But I digress though, so, we went our separate ways that day after he dropped me off at home.

Then unfortunately because of some ungodly counsel from a friend of mine I went out of town to Florida with Dre still! Bad idea! I repeat it was a bad idea. That trip was one of the worst little vacations I've ever had. I was sad the whole time. He didn't really care that I was sad because unfortunately he lacked the capacity to empathize. If it wasn't something that happened to hurt his feelings, it didn't register.

So, we came back and continued to date and fornicate. I'm mentioning that for a reason because I'm going somewhere with this part of my story. One time in particular he was not being careful and didn't use the rhythm method. That same morning after he had dropped me off to work, we had a conversation about what happened. He had all of this to say how it was not the right time for us to be having a baby and this and that. So, he decided and I went along with it that I would take a Plan B (morning after) pill. I was sooo against it. Everything in me did not want to because I just don't believe in it. I was out there being rebellious, but I had my convictions and abortion was one of them.

It was I believe the end of March of 2015 and I went out to party for my cousin Drina's birthday. This was a few weeks or so after I had taken the Plan B pill. Drina had come to visit me for her birthday and mine also. So, we went out to party, and I had been drinking and fell asleep standing up in the strip club. I believe I was leaning on something while standing. Nevertheless, after that weekend of her birthday I realized that my period had not come. So, I went to get a pregnancy test from the store and I took the test. And yep, you guessed it. The pregnancy test was positive. I was pregnant. Now during this time Dre and I were not on the best terms. This happened often. We were always arguing about something. Even so, I still let him know I was pregnant. I was actually happy about the pregnancy. I love kids and always wanted children of my own.

Anyway, maybe a week goes by and I start to spot blood. I was also having some pain at that time too in my abdomen. So, I went to the emergency room. I let them know I was pregnant, and they gave me I.V. fluids because, apparently, I was also dehydrated. Then they ordered an ultrasound, and they did it vaginally because I was very early on in the pregnancy. I believe I was about 6.5 weeks pregnant. The ultrasound I believe couldn't find a heartbeat or they couldn't find the embryo sac. I can't remember but they kept running blood tests. They specifically checked my HCG levels, which is the name of the hormone that shows up in your blood when you are pregnant. My HCG levels were in alignment with how far along I was but couldn't find the baby.

They finally did an ultrasound again and it showed that the embryo had implanted on the outside of my lower right part of my cervix. This meant that I had a cervical ectopic pregnancy. The pregnancy was no longer viable. So, I went through a course of blood draws and they gave me a radiation drug called methotrexate to stop the baby from growing. I'm not afraid of needles y'all but it was the thought of what they were putting in my body and the purpose of it. To ultimately end my pregnancy because unfortunately it was a life-or-death situation. The injections of the medication didn't work, and the baby was doing what he or she was supposed to do which was grow and that led to the hospital keeping me overnight and monitoring for complications.

Then in the morning they performed an interventional radiology procedure and observed me for a few hours and sent me home. Now I know you all are probably wondering where Dre was in all of this. Well, he was around but he was just not present during this very traumatic time of my life. He was preoccupied. The night they kept me he did not stay with me. He actually said that he couldn't. I knew in my heart what was up though. That he wanted to be with some other woman seeing that I was hospitalized. I want to say this, I'm not trying to make Dre out to be a villain I'm just sharing my story, Amen. I said all that to say y'all that I went through this experience of losing my first child by myself with just a very sweet Registered Nurse holding my hand during the interventional radiology procedure. She was an angel unaware for sure that morning!

After this tragic ordeal with losing my first child y'all I was devastated. I wanted a child so desperately after this.

I thought Lord, how can you give me a child and then in a blink of an eye the baby was gone. I say baby because life starts at conception! I believe the word of God!

> Before I formed thee in the belly I knew thee; and before thou camest forth out of the womb I sanctified thee, and I ordained thee a prophet unto the nations.
>
> *Jeremiah 1:5 KJV*

There isn't any confusion over this way, Amen!! So, as I stated, I desperately wanted a baby now. I was still in rebellion and no ladies I did not break up with Dre after this. I know I know, the Tom Foolery!!

Therefore, I continued in sin and also mourned the loss of our baby. In my desperation y'all I did what I knew best I cried out to God!! I worked as a Licensed Practical Nurse during this time and would just listen to K-Love on the radio to and from work. That is the Gospel station in Philly. I would pray on my way home from work every night and just listen to some of the men and women of God ministering and one evening on my way home I heard a man of God speaking of I believe Hannah in the bible and how she cried out to God to open up her womb!

So, I started praying right then that night. My prayer had shifted though. I prayed from a place of understanding that I needed to sacrifice my children and dedicate them to the Lord before they even were formed in my womb. And as I diligently prayed about this matter a few months later the Lord heard my humble cry! I lost my baby at the end of April 2016 and found out I was pregnant again October 2016. I shared that bit to give God the Glory and let you All know that God is more than faithful and able! Here I was not even living for God yet in His grace and mercy He saw fit to bless me not once but twice with two beautiful daughters.

During the first pregnancy I was still in a relationship with Dre. It was still toxic and came with so much drama. I believe he thought that once I got pregnant it would absolve him from me being worried about what he was doing. He cheated on me throughout that pregnancy and after the birth of our daughter Addison he continued to cheat. It was as if I was a single mom. During this time, I would go through a state of postpartum depression that took a different form than others. Which is why I didn't realize it until a few years later. I loved my daughter Addison but had lost the joy of doing things that I normally would enjoy doing. I didn't go places. I had no time set aside for myself. It wouldn't be until after my second child that I would find who I was but this time it wouldn't be my idea of who I was. Wait a minute though, let's not jump too far ahead.

So, after having Addison in July 2017 my life completely changed. I no longer had myself to think about but her also. She gave my life a whole new meaning. My relationship with Dre continued a downwards spiral. Then the unexpected happened! Well, I don't know how unexpected it was because unfortunately we were not practicing what the world calls "safe" sex. Yep, y'all girl was pregnant again and Addison was about 9 months old still nursing (breastfeeding) and all. I was like Lord, he got me again, no[lol]. I remember taking the pregnancy test at a good friend's house on Resurrection Sunday and that thang lit up like a Christmas tree. It didn't even need the five minutes it was supposed to normally take.

I remember deciding that I would tell Dre on Father's Day. And again, during this time we were on bad terms. So, some weeks passed, and I was at his aunt's place living because of some bad argument we had. It was one moment we were on the phone and somehow it came up during a discussion we were having. I was like well I'm pregnant again and to my surprise he suggested that I get an abortion. Of course I told him he had lost his mind! I wasn't aborting my baby. So, he slightly came to his senses, and we were good for about a month or two.

Then it was Addison's first birthday July 2018, and I was about three months pregnant by now. Dre and I got into a physical fight because I believe we were arguing about different women he was entertaining again. I was fed up y'all and he didn't like that I had something to say about it. So, we ended up fighting on her birthday that year and then we broke up from that moment. We still continued to be in communication because of Addison but that was it. I was so distraught about it honestly. I was like I did not sign up for this single mom life. I also had gone back to work as a nurse and worked up until my due date of my second daughter.

During the time of us being separated I was going through what I didn't know at the time was spiritual warfare. I remember a good friend of mine that was also a fellow nurse, Jamal, inviting me out to lunch and telling me that the devil was attacking me. My first thought and in my ignorance, I said why me? Not knowing the enemy was trying to take me out and I also had open doors. I'll talk about open doors here soon.

Nevertheless, I spent the next 6 months or so pregnant and alone. It was just me and God and my baby Addison. I promise you till this day if I didn't have some sort of foundation and knowledge of God I would not be here (living) let alone where I am now. The devil had it out for me.

February of 2019 comes, and I have my checkup appointment and in the middle of the night I went into labor. I drove myself to the Birthing Center in Bryn Mawr, PA and called Dre to let him know to meet me there. He came there and was supportive through the birthing process. I had a difficult Birth with my baby girl Aaurlow. She was a big baby, and I was tiny. I labored 12 hours with her unmedicated and then boom she was here.

After the birth of Aaurlow February 2019, Dre and I got back together. Whew, I know, I know an emotional Rollercoaster!! Yet there we were! So, we're back together and it was much of the same thing as before. Arguing about women and I really just didn't trust him. So, I believe it was around November of 2019 and I'd had enough so we broke up AGAIN!! I went to visit my hometown St. Louis for about a month and a half. Honestly when I left, I had no intention of coming back to Philly. That just goes to show how bad it was between the two of us.

After some thought though I flew back at the end of December. When I got back Dre wanted to talk and so we did over the phone only. He wanted me to meet him somewhere and I was like I don't know. I talked to a friend about it and was like sis, if he tries to propose to me, I'm gonna say no. At least that's what the wise Tammira thought[lol]. So, I met him at said location and sure enough y'all he asked me to marry him and I... drum roll please, I foolishly said Yes! Then things got better...Nope! Keep reading on to see what happens next.

Chapter 7
Unveiled

We got engaged and then moved back in with one another that February of 2020. And we All know what happened then. Yep, the Corona virus had them locking everything down that March 2020. So, we were locked in together and around this same time the Lord began to open my spiritual eyes. God was removing the scales from my eyes. All the while my relationship with Dre was in a downward spiral. We were arguing more and fighting, sometimes physically. It was just a toxic, unhealthy mess from the pit of hell.

Then one day in around April or so of that year, I had an unusual encounter with God. He divinely placed a YouTube video from Marcus Rogers in my path. I was downstairs and Dre was upstairs taking a nap with the kids and then the volume on the TV started going up and down. So, I'm yelling upstairs to ask if he is messing with the TV. He never answered me. Then I went into the kitchen and all of a sudden, I heard my phone fall off of the couch onto the floor. I walked over and looked because it was odd to me seeing that where my phone was placed on the couch there is no way it could've just fallen off. Might I remind you I was the only one downstairs.

So, I'm like, "hold up what just happened here." I knew it was supernatural at that moment. I picked my phone up off of the floor and the first thing I saw on it was a video from Marcus Rogers about Trump and some things to come. I remember he was sitting on the side of a tub and running water in it. From that moment I started to watch him and listen to what the Lord was saying through him. The Lord used him in that season to draw me out of the darkness and into the marvelous light. I wasn't out just yet though. I had many strongholds that needed to be broken off. The closer I got to the Lord in 2020 was the further Dre and I got from one another and the more we fought.

It was in July 2020 after my oldest daughter Addison's birthday, and we got into a huge argument, and I decided ok no for real enough is enough. Talk about demonic cycles. I had given him back the ring and moved into his aunt's place that she rented out to him. While there I started noticing that I was having nightmares more frequently. I remember specifically that I was dreaming and then I opened my eyes, and it was like some type of figure coming out of the living room into my room. I was so scared, and I already was dealing with fear. It was after that moment that I began to be so afraid that I couldn't sleep.

Then I reached out to my brother and my sis Alex from back home about it. My brother's wife then sends me a message and a YouTube video of a prayer against sleep paralysis and night terrors. I prayed along with it. Then my sis Alex sent me a YouTube video of a woman of God Nia-Cerise who had come out of a life of witchcraft. In the video she explained that it was demons (incubus and succubus) that were holding you down when the "sleep paralysis" happens. She also went on to say that the reason they had access and could attack you, was because of open doors. I'm like, open doors? All my doors closed, no but for real there is such a thing in the Spirit. An open door is any form of sin that you are doing knowingly or unknowingly. It can also be a door that someone in your bloodline opened. So if you are in fornication, masturbation (which is having sex with demons), rebellion (which is as the sin of witchcraft) 1 Samuel 15:23 and drunkenness. These are just some forms of open doors. And the one's named were some of the open doors I had, and the enemy was having a field day with the fact that I was ignorant to his devices.

From that moment on, after I watched that video I closed all known open doors. I stopped drinking, masturbating and cursing. And though I stopped those things I was still dealing with the tormenting spirit of fear. So, I was staying up until sunrise for about a month or so, give or take. This time was not wasted at all though. The Lord used what the enemy meant for evil for my good. When I would be up in the middle of the night, the Holy Spirit was teaching me to pray and intercede for my family and friends. I was praying all night and also able to see when the enemy tried to attack one of my daughters. She was sleeping next to me, and I believe I had briefly dozed off. The next thing I heard was Addison screaming and I looked over and something was pulling her towards the bottom of the bed. I began to pray and war and rebuke the devil and his minions in Jesus Name. Then I consoled her, and it was then that I began to come into the understanding that I had a real enemy I was dealing with.

Also, during this time, I was still single, and Dre would rarely come to see the kids. This was one of the main things I was struggling with too at the time, was to remain out of that toxic and unhealthy relationship. The thing that made it hard was the fact that I had a soul tie with him. A soul tie is the result of us having sex with someone that we are not married too. You can also form a soul tie with someone that you are just friends with, but the most common way is through sexual intercourse. The reason is because sex was designed for marriage. The two become one as they make that covenant with one another. Therefore, because you are not married to the person every time you have sex with them your two souls are joined.

Then you take a piece of their soul, and they take a piece of yours when you are no longer together. Also, whatever demons they have, they are transferred during the act of fornication. Now that I've explained that, back to the story.

So, because of the soul tie mentioned, I thought that I was completely finished with Dre but the enemy had other plans. We began communicating more and he came over one time to give me the ring back. He said all of these things that still didn't have me convinced but at that time it all sounded good. I didn't want the girls to not have their dad around and I desired to be a wife. There was a catch to it also, when it came to us getting back together. I had let him know that I had made a vow to the Lord that I was not going to have sex again until I got married. I think that was some incentive for him to want to continue on with everything but who knows. Also, I forgot to mention that during all of this I was in the process of getting ready to move into my own apartment with the girls. I had to get out of his aunt's place as soon as possible.

Unveiled Part Two

So that September myself and the girls moved out to the outskirts of Philadelphia into an apartment. Again, as I said, Dre and I had gotten back together and by now we had set a date for that October of 2020. We would elope first on October 3 and then have a ceremony in my hometown Saint Louis

Missouri on November 14, 2020. Y'all the warfare that I experienced from the time of getting back together with Dre and leading up to the actual wedding day was so extreme. The sad part of that was me ignorantly thinking that it was the devil trying to keep us from getting married. Nope, sike! It was the Lord trying to prevent me from making a terrible decision that would later lead to more warfare.

Nevertheless, we got married on those dates, first in front of a Justice of Peace and then in front of our loved ones in my hometown. We returned back to Pennsylvania and the warfare continued. We argued about nonsense. One of the things that we argued about most was the election and God. The devil had placed blinders on him in regards to what the government was doing during that time and also in regards to God. I was going deeper in my relationship with God, and he couldn't understand why I wouldn't do the things I used to do. See I had the understanding that I was a new creature.

> Therefore if any man be in Christ, he is a new creature: old things are passed away; behold, all things are become new.
>
> *2 Corinthians 5:17 KJV*

This concept was something that he had a very hard time comprehending. That didn't matter to me though because I was sold out to Christ. I was reading my word, praying and worshiping all day throughout my home. So much so that my apartment housed the Kabod (Glory) of God. I knew this because every time Dre would come over the spirit of anger and rage would eventually manifest itself.

It got to a point where he could only stay for about twenty minutes before the unclean spirits would manifest and cause something to happen between us. It was leading up to this moment that I prayed and prayed and sought wise counsel about what to do with the marriage. I mean I went into warfare intercession for his salvation until I came to the realization by way of Holy Spirit that I am no Savior. There is only one name by which one can be saved, that name is Jesus.

Neither is there salvation in any other: for there is none other name under heaven given among men, whereby we must be saved.

Acts 4:12 KJV [12]

So, once I was able to grasp this revelation, my prayer changed. I asked the Lord what He wanted me to do because Dre didn't want to live under the same roof, and I knew there was infidelity going on. Therefore, after much prayer and wrestling with God and my flesh, I filed for a divorce. I wept as I gave them the paperwork at that office on April 19, 2021. I then began to deep dive into the word of God, the Bible. As soon as I decided to start reading the Bible, that same night I got attacked in my sleep by the devil. I was asleep for all of ten minutes y'all and then I felt a demon try to hold me down or stop me from speaking. I simply woke up and laughed and rebuked the devil in Jesus Name. My exact words were, "Oh you Big Mad"? I went back to sleep with a smile on my face and slept like a baby.

See the enemy doesn't come with new tactics y'all he just tries to come a different way. I had already been delivered from the spirit of fear in my sleep after I moved to that new apartment. Therefore, when the devil and his minions came, that time I was delivered and equipped. I wasn't ignorant to satan's devices. That's why I just rebuked that thing and went on to sleep peacefully. Holy Spirit had taught me my authority in Jesus Christ, and I started walking in it. It was around this same time that I started to feel an unction from the Holy Spirit that my time was up in Pennsylvania. It had been 8 years that I lived there, and I knew that it was honestly a year past the time I should've been gone.

So, following my flesh and not the Holy Spirit I ended up in Canal Winchester Ohio. There was also some prophetic witchcraft sprinkled up in there from a friend that I thought was real Man of God. Unfortunately, though he was under the influence of a seducing and jezebel spirit, I digress. So, the girls and I were now in Ohio. It was December of 2021 and bitter cold for real. We attended a ministry out there immediately. Once we got there, the Holy Spirit started to increase and sharpen my gift of discerning of spirits. I noticed right away the spirit of religion, self-righteousness and pride were at work in that church. It wouldn't be too long after that, roughly six months, that Holy Spirit would reveal to me that a strong spirit of prophetic witchcraft and a spirit of jezebel were at work in the ministry. These two are really one in the same.

    I immediately stopped attending the church. Right after I stopped attending the church I received a few interesting phone calls and messages from the Pastor and a few members. Then I had a vision in the night when I was sleeping and then I opened my eyes and in the corner of my room towards the ceiling I saw what looked to be a portal that looked like an eye. I immediately started to pray and blind and bind all monitoring spirits and close every portal the enemy had tried to open. Yea I don't play with the devil over here. I give him no place, Amen.

Then after that I also saw a black spider in my bed. Yes, complete witchcraft. The devil was mad because his plot and schemes had been uncovered. That place was meant to completely kill me spiritually, but God! I was able to take all of what I learned that season as a lesson and the Lord continued to train me up spiritually.

By July of 2022, after some warfare and divine intervention from

God I had been given the green light to move to Houston Texas. I had become an online member of a ministry that was based in Houston. Therefore, the Lord had said to move there so that I could fellowship in person. The girls, myself and a dear sister in Christ of mine hopped on the highway on July 7, 2022. We made it into Houston at around 4:00 a.m. on July 8, 2022. Only the Holy Spirit could've gotten us there because the Lord knows y'all girl was tired! Nevertheless, we made it in to H-Town! Welcome to my promise land.

Chapter 8
Promise Fulfilled

Yay!! We arrived in Houston Texas! At the time when we arrived, I had a sister in Christ that we were able to live with. We ended up staying with her for about seven months. That time was a very humbling and eye-opening experience. The girls and I went from sleeping in a very spacious two-bedroom apartment in Ohio to now sleeping on an air mattress in the living room of a one-bedroom apartment with two other people. Not to mention the spiritual aspect of it all. Unfortunately, I'd gone from one form of witchcraft to another. We as believers must not be ignorant to satan's devices. I know I mentioned it in a previous chapter, but I can't say it enough. The devil doesn't come with anything new, and he likes to use those that are closest to you when they have open doors. I spoke about open doors in a previous chapter also.

Nevertheless, we were in an environment where we were being manipulated, controlled and intimidated. And manipulation is one of the strongest forms of witchcraft. The fact that I discerned something was off but didn't act on it until later is how a lot of believers in Christ are. I let my love for this person almost completely get rid of my discernment. In this particular season though, Holy Spirit again reminded me that I hear His voice very clearly and that it is wise not to ignore it. I wanted to pause there for a minute to share that wisdom with you all.

Now it's February of 2023 and I found an apartment by God's grace and removed myself from that very unhealthy environment. So now the girls and I are in our own place and comfortable for the most part. We didn't have much because what I didn't sale in Ohio I just simply left or gave away. By God's grace though we were comfortable and our pastors at the time donated a few mattresses and a table to us. So, we had essentials, Amen. I was so grateful for all of the help and prayers.

I remember during this time I was instructed to move in silence. There is much wisdom in listening to the voice of God. Everyone does not need to know your every move. It can bring on unwanted spiritual warfare. You're getting hit on all sides by the devil and wondering why. It's most likely because you are giving information right to his minions, demons. Some people are asking because they are going to genuinely pray for you. The others are asking so that they can prey on you!! We as the Body of Christ must lean into the voice of Holy Spirit and listen as well as obey Him.

Now did I still come up against some spiritual warfare? Yes, but it was because of the transition and the devil not wanting me to progress and not from me talking too much. Let me not forget to mention that during all these trials, tribulations and testing of my Faith that I was still sending paperwork back and forth to get the divorce finalized. Yes, it had been almost two years. The ex, had decided that he wasn't going to sign the paperwork. It was a form of control and the plan of the devil to try to keep prophecy from being fulfilled. God's word never falls to the ground though.

So, it was at the end of February around the 28th I believe when I got the call from the woman at the office in Pennsylvania. She said that she had great news and that the divorce decree had been finalized! I cried tears of relief and joy. I want to make it very clear that I am not an advocate for divorce. I have to say this because I know how the Saints are, and I don't want my words twisted. This is a message I sent to a woman of God, "I just wanted to give a praise report that after almost two years of warfare with my now ex-husband as of today because Jesus did it, my divorce is finalized!!!!! Hallelujah, I don't rejoice in the divorce. I rejoice because the covenant that was from the pit of hell is broken off of me and my bloodline. Now I patiently await my God ordained spouse. God knew what He was doing." I say all of that to say that I'm for marriage because the God I serve honors covenant. He is a covenant keeping God! As this part of my story continues to unfold, you'll see just how much He showed up and showed out on His daughter's behalf.

    The next six months would be difficult but by God's grace I would see His hands in it all. During this time, I quit my job as a Unit Manager Nurse because of the stress of the position and the danger that the facility was putting the residents in. I know I know; it doesn't sound like it was the wisest thing to do. Looking back though, I would've done it the same honestly.

    Nevertheless, I was without a job by March and doing some as needed nursing assignments. It was difficult to keep food on the table, but the Lord always provided for us. I began to stand on the scripture:

> I have been young, and now am old; Yet have I not seen the righteous forsaken, nor his seed begging bread.
>
> *Psalm 37:25 KJV*

I had moments of discouragement, disappointment and discontent but I was never defeated! I knew that I served a God that always showed up for His children. As much as the enemy wanted to kill my Faith it didn't work. The exact opposite happened actually. My Faith just grew and grew! The Holy Spirit was showing me that indeed I do have the gift of Faith. No devil in hell could stop what God was about to do in my life.

Now the end of August came, and my lease was up at my current apartment. My daughters and I then moved into another apartment. It was by the grace of God that we were able to find one seeing that my credit was not the best. Our God is rich in mercy though and always has a plan. I was shown favor at an apartment complex by this gracious woman named, Ruth. Now hold on tight y'all because from the moment we moved there, things moved with supernatural speed. Ok wait, no it was actually after I was obedient to the Lord in shifting from the ministry, I moved out to Houston to be a part of to the ministry He had strategically planted for myself and many others in the heart of Sunnyside Houston.

So, we shifted to the ministry, RIG Global in September. Yes, it's a shameless plug! IYKYK! Once I started getting plugged into the church by going out to Street Church and volunteering in the children's ministry the Lord just moved so miraculously. It was as if there started to be a supernatural acceleration in every aspect of my life. Also Ms. Lisanne had added me to the RIG Women's chat where I could get plugged in and connected. Shortly after that the Lord created a divine appointment. I was at the right place at the right time. And had I not shifted ministries when Holy Spirit told me to, I would have missed

God!! My constant prayer has been, "Lord let me be at the right place at the right time and never at the wrong place at the wrong time." Praise God that the effectual fervent prayers of the righteous availeth much.

It was October 6, 2023, when I received a message in the women's group chat for my church RIG Global. Ms. Lisanne asked if there would be anyone interested in volunteering for a Chaplain Program in schools here In Texas. I immediately responded to her message in the chat and said that I would love to. So, she messaged me directly and gave me the individual's name, Joshua, and said he would be contacting me soon. Shortly after that I received a call from Joshua and we started out talking about the Chaplain program, but the conversation shifted quickly, and we began to just talk about all things God. We ended up on the phone for two plus hours y'all!! I was left asking Holy Spirt, "Who is this Man of God?". I needed answers because I was intrigued by our conversation. I just knew we were supposed to be connected but just didn't know to what extent.

So, we continued to text after that. I was sending the Man of God food reels because he had told me he was only eating fish and veggies. Also, I'm a foodie but that's neither here nor there [lol]! Then it was like a few weeks later that he said that he would be at my church RIG Global and so I was like ok,

"I'll see you there then". I got to church, and we are messaging during service about what was being preached (Don't come for me Saints). It was a great word too. Then the service was over, and we met each other for the first time. I was nervous and also in a bit of a hurry because I had to get my girls from children's church. So, we exchanged a very awkward hi and then parted ways.

    We continued to message one another everyday just about. All the while I'm in my prayer closet asking Holy Spirit like who is this Man of God and where does he fit in my life? The Holy Spirit was not answering me y'all! [LOL] This was because I had heard him right the first time [lbs]!

Some weeks passed and then he had messaged me one day and asked if I would lead prayer on one day of the week for Houston Prayer 24/7. I hesitated when he asked because anyone who knows me knows that normally, Tammira, doesn't want to lead anything. I like to serve in the background (The Lord is changing that though). I knew it was Holy spirit using Joshua to pull me out of my comfort zone, so I said sure. I ended up choosing Monday because I had various other things I was doing throughout the week.

    The first time on the prayer call it was supposed to be myself, Joshua and another sister, but she never showed up. So, it was just him and I praying every Monday. And from that first call we would pray and then because I have the gift of gab [lol], we would end up on the phone for hours afterwards. We would be talking about everything, and I do mean everything. Holy Spirit had us on a fast track of getting to know one another. We shared our testimonies with one another of how we came to Christ and other life lessons. I remember thinking a few times like Holy Spirit why is he telling me All of his business. Nevertheless, we were truly developing a beautiful friendship.

Throughout these times I would still be praying and asking the Lord about Joshua and his purpose in my life. The Lord wasn't saying much but I just had a knowing. There were at least three occasions where Joshua asked me what Holy Spirit had shown me about him and I replied, "Nothing that I have been given permission to share". So, y'all I said that because I had felt like Holy Spirit had told me that he was my husband, but I wasn't about to be out of order and say that. The bible says, "He that findeth a wife findeth a good thing and obtaineth favor from the Lord". That's a little nugget for all my single Women of God out there. DO NOT tell that man he is your husband even if Holy Spirit reveals it to you first. When wisdom speaks listen, AMEN!

In conjunction with Holy Spirit giving me the unction that Joshua was the one, I had also been given a prophetic word in January of that year,

2023. The Lord had said that He was going to be connecting me with the man that was going to be my husband before the end of the year. So I had warred with that word for ten months, but God.

Okay y'all...whew. Hang in there. It's getting to the good part. Well all the parts are good but anyways [lol]. So fast forward to the end of November and I joined TYOTB Fast with Prophetess Tiphani Montgomery...IYKYK! The fast was for 25 days ending on the 21st of December. Joshua and I are still talking every day, but the Man of God hadn't said not one word about being interested in me or anything [lol]. I mean it should have been obvious, but it wasn't. So, I'm like Holy Spirit, I like him but if I'm not supposed to like him take these feelings away. I wanted to be in alignment with the will of God for my life.

Around this same time Holy Spirit had been impressing upon me for weeks to wake up early in the morning and pray. I briefly mentioned it to Joshua and then I began to wake up and pray. Then maybe a day or so afterwards Joshua said, "let's just pray together at that same time that way you have accountability and you're not doing it alone". We started praying together and it was at this point ya girl was just swept off of her feet, highkey[lbs].

Then fast forward to the last week of that fast in December and I saw this post on IG about this Nigerian

Minister of music that would be in Houston. I love to worship so I just sent it to Joshua like yooo I'm mad excited about this event and will most likely go. Joshua was like that the worship event was close to him and that he would come also. Ya'll, I needed clarification cause listen, you know [lol]. So, I asked him "You gone be where?" and he just simply said the worship event.

So, y'all I'm hyped high-key because I was looking forward to spending time with him. At the same time, I also needed him to actually ask me out or else I was like we just going as friends. Listen up, take notes women of God. Let him be intentional and make that first move. Anyways, so then I got an opportunity to go serve in Dallas with my church RIG Global and I went there on that Friday December 22nd. I get there and I'm serving but Joshua and I weren't messaging as much because he knew I was busy. Then I'm in the service and I get this feeling of like I miss him. It literally came out of nowhere. So, I'm like Holy Spirit what's this cause he's just my friend and I brush it off because of course I can't text him that. The night ends and we're all praying at like 3 am with my church family and I call Joshua and he's on the line praying also.

Saturday comes, December 23rd ... I'm mentioning the dates because trust me, they matter. So, it's Saturday and we drive back to Houston. Joshua tells me to text him when I get home. I texted him when I got home but then he called me and we talked per usual. Then something happened to where he was getting ready to say something but didn't. I felt some weight behind what he was going to say. So, ladies you know how we are [lol]...I let a little time pass in conversation and then asked him what he was about to say. I was like, "You not gone just try to skip pass that like I forgot". Then he says, "Can I take you out"? and then I say, "I thought you'd never ask". Then I went on to tell him, that is what I thought we were doing, and he was like he knows but he wanted to be intentional. Then he said two more statements that I knew was Holy Spirit speaking, "Oh ye of little faith" and "Are you ready?" I'm sitting on the side of my bed in a Holy Awe of God because I knew I heard Holy Spirit correctly. So, I'm like ok Holy Spirit we will start courting and you just have your way. Holy Spirit definitely had other plans [lol].

The worship event was on December 26th and we met up at the event space and had a blessed time in the Lord!! Then we went to get tacos and ended the night with a side hug (leave some room for Jesus lol) and parted ways. Then it was while we were on the phone and I wasn't even on the highway yet and Joshua goes, "So when is our wedding date?", y'all it was then that Holy Spirit was like, "I told you". So, whereas I thought we would court one another for a little while Holy Spirit was like nope, supernatural speed. After that first date it was like the Lord just blew on our relationship.

January 2024 came, and we both did a water fast from the 1st of that month until January 14th. While on the fast the Lord told us that things would happen fast. How many of you know when God says a thing to believe it? Things moved so fast between us once we were in agreement with God. Amos 9:13 was made manifest in our lives. The next step was for us to go ahead and tell our immediate family. So, Joshua took the leap and told his parents and siblings. His mom asked if he was sure and Joshua said, "It's All God."

Then it was my turn to tell my family. For me though, I was hesitant because I didn't want seeds of doubt to be sown. Nevertheless, I reached out to my family and let them know we were getting married. Their initial response was, "you getting what?" I was like you heard me correctly[lol]. Then their next questions were where did he come from and how long have you known him. I answered the questions and then also let them know that all of those details didn't really matter. God had ordained it from the beginning of the earth. So, my mom was like "okay" but there was some doubt there. I made sure not let too much be said that was contrary to what God said because I didn't want to second guess God. There are people with good intentions but if it goes against what God has said that means it's coming from the flesh. Also, the enemy will come anyway that he can. I just wanted to say that to encourage some of you who God has spoken to and you are waiting for confirmations. The Lord says that it was not a conference call when He gave you the word and or when He called you. People will most likely not understand or agree with your obedience, but it is better to obey God than man. Also, there is safety in discretion.

    The reason that my family was like where did Joshua come from was because no one knew of him. I had been given strict instructions from the Holy Spirit not to tell anyone about him. I mean I never mentioned his name or anything. Now I know why the Holy Spirit told me to move that way. It was because of the amount of warfare, word curses and seeds of doubt that would have been sown. When it's a God thing the devil will attempt to steal, kill and destroy.

So, our families were now aware, and it was now time to choose a date for the wedding. We decided that we would pray about it of course, so we did. Then I was on my way home from church and the Holy Spirit dropped it in my spirit to mention it right then. So, I messaged the Man of God and asked what date the Lord gave him. I told him the Lord gave me March 24, 2024. He messaged me back "March 24, 2025". I was driving y'all and didn't take note that the year was different[lol]. Then it came time for us to sit down and plan the wedding, I looked at him and said, "okay March 24, 2024", as he was writing down the date. Y'all once I saw that 2025, I was like hold on what I did I miss[lol]. Then we sat right there and talked to Holy Spirit and He confirmed the date. It was all gas no breaks after that. Our heads were for sure on a swivel. I believe it was within a week or so after this that we would have a venue booked for 3.24.2024. Before January was finished, he bought us purity rings. I know I was caught off guard in the best way (Yes come along and start believing in love again with me). When he pulled that box out of his pocket I almost gut punched him y'all. A

Holy gut punch of course. Listen religious folks it's jokes, all jokes[lol]. No one got injured during the giving of the purity ring[haha].

It is now the month of February, and we are sending out invites and looking for cake shops. Our church RIG Global was having a marriage conference and I had registered us. The conference dates were February 16th and 17th. I was so hype about it. I was ready to lean in and glean, Amen. The first day of the conference was fire for fire! There were so many nuggets of wisdom given.

Then Saturday February 17th came, the second day of the conference. We left that afternoon during intermission to get food. Before we left, he said that he had a meeting with someone at 6pm. I wanted to know so bad who he had to meet with but the moment I got ready to ask I heard the Holy Spirit say no. Holy Spirit told me not to worry about it. Thank you God for the Holy Ghost and Praise God even the more that I obeyed. Had I not obeyed the voice of the Spirit of God I would have ruined everything because you guessed it, drum roll please. The Man of God proposed right in the foyer of our church. To my surprise, here it was all of these people here to celebrate me and the beautiful gift the Lord had given me. I'm still at a Holy Awe of God even as I write this. Never could I have imagined it playing out like this.

So, tears were shed and the amount of joy in that place was tangible! Only the Holy Spirit could have done it. Now the cat was out of the bag. Yes, it had been quiet as kept up until that day. As much as y'all girl had wanted to stay hidden, Holy Spirit decided to put me on full display. We were all over social media for that weekend alongside the hashtag, breakthrough. Next up was the big day. There was about a month from the formal proposal to the actual wedding date. The time was moving so fast!!

Next, I had an amazing Woman of God honor me and bless me by throwing me a bridal shower. What happened on that day March 17th was nothing short of God displaying His

Glory and His love toward me. The presence of the Holy Spirit was so thick in her house. It was something that I had never seen before. I mean truly miraculous. After the bridal shower the Woman of God, Quinity, said she had never experienced anything like it. I mean from the moment I walked into her house and these sisters in Christ adorned me with jewelry. I saw prophecy fulfilled.

Then prophecy went forth, prophetic worship and prophetic dance. I was so honored and humbled that they would want to celebrate me. I have always been used to celebrating other people and serving them in the background. So, when these women of God came out and treated me like a queen. I mean they treated me like who God sees me as, which is the daughter of a King! It really blessed me immeasurably. The way I cried most of that night. They were happy tears of course. I have cried many tears of sorrow and pain so this day and the days to come would be filled with so much joy. It would be Isaiah 61:3 made manifest,

> to appoint unto them that mourn in Zion, to give unto them beauty for ashes, the oil of joy for mourning, the garment of praise for the spirit of heaviness; that they might be called trees of righteousness, the planting of the LORD, that he might be glorified.
>
> *Isaiah 61:3 KJV [3]*

After the bridal shower we had a week until the day of the wedding. The days leading up to the wedding day that week were again glorious and miraculous! From being laid out prostrate in the presence of God to just soaking in His presence! Whew I'd do it a thousand times over.

Now it is the big day 3.24.2024 and our little family is getting prepared and ready to go to the venue. Everything moved seamlessly. I as the bride had so much help that day. My amazing sister in Christ Paige, whew I was about to drop a tear. May God richly bless her in Jesus Mighty Name Amen. And oh, did He! Moving right along though. So, from the moment I arrived at the venue I was told not to do much. I'm always trying to do for myself even when I have help around me[lol]. It was learned behavior and that day and leading up to it the Lord was teaching me how to receive.

The time had come that we had both waited for, me walking down the aisle. The door opens and the kids go before me and then I walk through the doors. I looked to my right and immediately started crying once I saw my Father walking up to greet me. Then I gather myself and see all of these people standing up to watch me walk down the aisle as I hear Yeshua playing over the loudspeaker. I prayed and sang the whole way to the altar.

Then I look over and the Man of God the Lord hand-picked and set apart for me was standing there weeping as he waited for me. My dad then handed me over to my Man of God, Joshua. We said our vows, I do's and sealed it with a kiss. Might I add our first kiss at that. Then we washed one another's feet, this had to be one of the most intimate moments ever. It's also something that we still do even to this day.

We then ended the ceremony with dancing and fellowship with our family and friends. It was the most Holy Spirit filled wedding that I've been to. Actually, let me take that back. It was the only one I have been to (God is doing a new thing though). Our wedding day was a day that many prophecies were fulfilled. And God's children and even those that don't know Him as Abba Father got to witness the hand of God working in and through our lives. To be a sign and a wonder for His Glory!! But the rest is Our Story for His Glory!!

Really quickly I want to shed light on a few things in this part of the book. I received a word in January 2023 from a beautiful Woman of God in whom ministry I serve on that I would meet the Man of God that would be my husband before the year was out. All those months passed by y'all, but I held on to that word from the Lord. There were times when the enemy would try to discourage me cause I didn't see a man in sight. Still, I would pray as the Lord led for him and his family. The Lord would show me things about my God ordained spouse and I would pray into it. I did what people may call

CRAZY acts of FAITH because I know I heard God, and I believed God. I bought my wedding dress in December of 2022 because the Holy Spirit told me to go in Faith and try on dresses. To my surprise I found one that same day. I stood on Luke 1:45 And blessed is she that believed: for there shall be a performance of those things which were told her from the Lord. And the last two that I will leave you all with is...

> so shall my word be that goeth forth out of my mouth: it shall not return to me void, but it shall accomplish that which I please, and it shall prosper in the thing whereto I sent it.
>
> *Isaiah 55:11*

Every sure word of prophecy spoken over your life shall come to pass because His word never returns back to Him void. It will come to pass and that's in every area of your life. So be encouraged by our love story that was completely orchestrated by God himself. Lastly, we were both chasing after God and He connected us only how He could. This is truly a Matthew 6:33 testimony amongst other things. Matthew 6:33 But seek ye first the kingdom of God, and His righteousness; and all these things shall be added unto you. As we are chasing after God and the things of God (and His righteousness… let's not forget this part) He has added and will continue to add All the other things unto us.

God really has done a thing, and words truly fail me when I think of spending the rest of my life with Joshua. Who am I that God is mindful of me. What is my house? The girls and I are truly blessed, and God is the best matchmaker hands down!! Trust God with this area of your life and watch HIM blow your mind!! Singing, Jesus Iye!!

Ps- be on the lookout for our wedding video and full testimony on YouTube. Who knows, there may even be a documentary/short film. God bless you All!!

Made in the USA
Middletown, DE
31 October 2024